Contents

How to Use This Book

Vocabulary Development offers learners the opportunity to improve their language arts skills through age-appropriate activities that were created to meet the curriculum used in schools nationwide. These activities are based on the standards of the International Reading Association (IRA) with a focus on vocabulary skills such as word recognition, contextualization, word structure, and word identification. These skills are an integral part of a successful writing and reading comprehension program for fifth graders. *Vocabulary Development* is a resource that not only hones language arts skills, but also makes learning exciting and fun.

Vocabulary Development is comprised of six sections: Antonyms and Synonyms, Word Meaning, Decoding Words, Origins, Figurative Expressions, and Vocabulary Helpers. Each section provides activities that are directly related to improving vocabulary development skills. Clear directions and skill definitions accompany each activity.

Antonyms and Synonyms

The skills practiced in this section concentrate on understanding the meanings of like and opposite words. Your learners will gain a better understanding of how to identify words.

Word Meaning

This section provides learners with the opportunity to identify words by understanding the context in which the word appears in a sentence. The different activities in this section help learners expand their vocabulary.

Decoding Words

The use of prefixes and suffixes in this section allows the learner to better understand the meaning of words. The learner can then begin to identify new word meanings based on his or her knowledge of both prefixes and suffixes.

Origins

Being able to identify the origins of certain words will provide the learner with ways to successfully identify unknown words. These activities will also allow the learner to increase his or her word usage skills.

2

Figurative Expressions

The reading comprehension skills in this section will provide the learner with the tools required to understand reading materials. The focus on similes and metaphors gives the learner a chance to find new ways of expressing him- or herself while focusing on writing activities.

Vocabulary Helpers

Learning to use a dictionary and thesaurus provides the foundation for success in any language arts program. This section provides learners with activities that encourage familiarity with these important reading tools.

Skills Correlation Guide

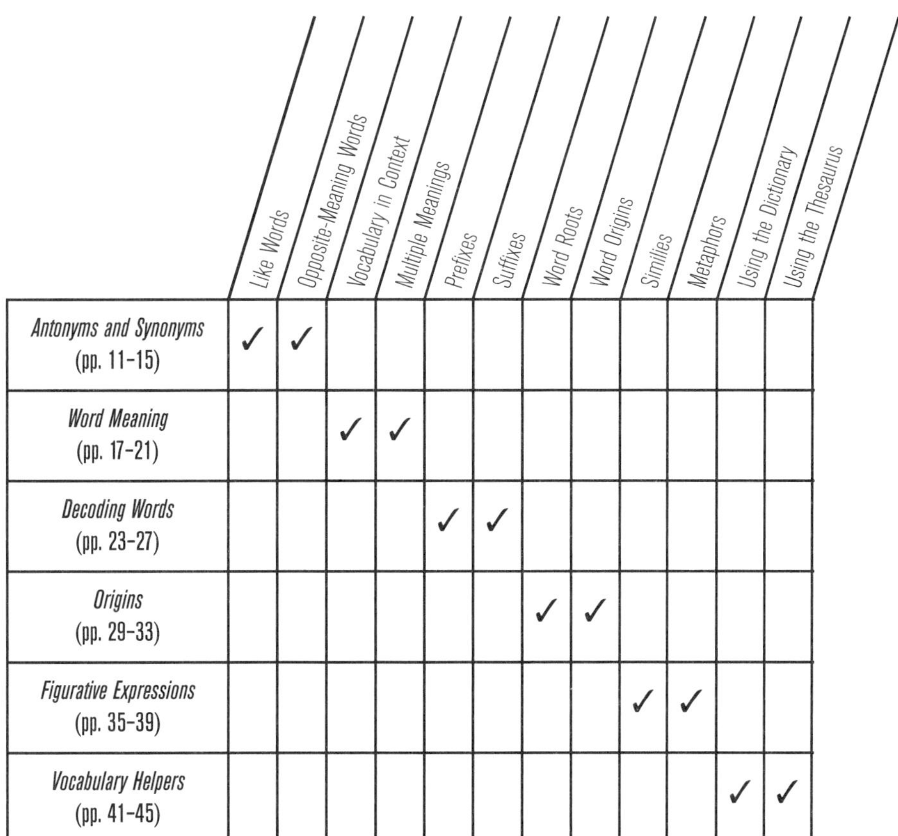

	Like Words	Opposite-Meaning Words	Vocabulary in Context	Multiple Meanings	Prefixes	Suffixes	Word Roots	Word Origins	Similies	Metaphors	Using the Dictionary	Using the Thesaurus
Antonyms and Synonyms (pp. 11–15)	✓	✓										
Word Meaning (pp. 17–21)			✓	✓								
Decoding Words (pp. 23–27)					✓	✓						
Origins (pp. 29–33)							✓	✓				
Figurative Expressions (pp. 35–39)									✓	✓		
Vocabulary Helpers (pp. 41–45)											✓	✓

The activities featured in this book are level U according to guidelines set by Fountas and Pinnell.

Name ________________________

Like Words

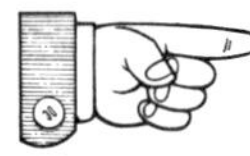 **Directions: Circle the word that means the same thing as the bold word in the sentence.**

1. She **cherished** her new puppy.

   adored   hated

2. The **discussion** was about schoolwork.

   fight   conversation

3. They **hauled** away the furniture.

   moved   emptied

4. He **appreciated** the good work.

   valued   commissioned

5. The **blossoms** were pretty.

   flowers   choice

4

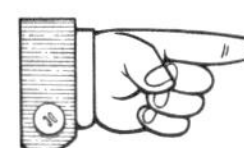

Name ______________________________

Multiple Meanings

Directions: Draw a line from each set of descriptions to the word that best matches it.

The space in a building between two floors

Something that can be read in a book

bank

A group that plays live music

Something that people wear in their hair

snap

A dog might do this if he's angry.

It is used to close things.

band

A river has one of these.

It is a place to put your money.

story

When you write your name you do this.

You can read this on a wall.

sign

Name ______________________

Suffixes

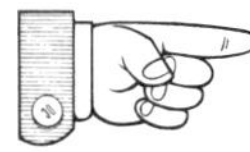 **Directions: Fill in the blanks from the suffix choices in the box to best complete the sentences.**

ful	ly	er	able

1. What she said was **question**____________.

2. The task took **consider**____________ effort.

3. He was **doubt**____________ that it would work out.

4. The cookies are in the **contain**____________.

5. She spoke **free**____________ about her feelings.

6

Name ______________________________

Roots

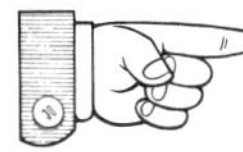 **Directions: Look at the underlined word in each sentence below. Then write the root of the word on the line provided.**

1. She was a great <u>musician</u>. ______________________________

2. Listen to the <u>commentator</u>. ______________________________

3. Her dress was <u>informal</u>. ______________________________

4. We bought them from a <u>peddler</u>. ______________________________

5. The fox used a good deal of <u>trickery</u> to escape the hunter.

____

Name ___________________________

Similes

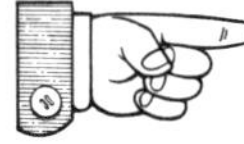 **Directions: Circle the sentences that use a simile.**

1. Deb was as funny as a clown.

2. The rainbow beamed in the sky.

3. Their house was like a museum.

4. The eagle soared as fast as a jet.

5. The rain was beating like a drum.

6. The cave was a doorway into another land.

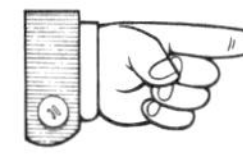

Vocabulary Helpers

Name ______________________________

Using the Dictionary

Directions: Put the following words in alphabetical order.

perfume	former	assemble	abandon	district
dispute	framework	prairie	preserve	

1. ______________________________

2. ______________________________

3. ______________________________

4. ______________________________

5. ______________________________

6. ______________________________

7. ______________________________

8. ______________________________

9. ______________________________

9

**For *Antonyms and Synonyms*
(pp. 11–15)**

Background

• Understanding synonyms and antonyms helps learners build on their knowledge of word definitions. As learners master the activities in this section, they expand on their vocabulary. A fuller vocabulary will help learners to write in a less repetitive manner.

Homework Helper

• Write a list of prefixes that the learners can use to change the meaning of a word, such as *un* or *in*. Then have the learners list as many words as they can that can be made into their own antonyms by adding the given prefix.

Research-based Activity

• Have the learners choose a paragraph from one of their favorite books. Ask them to pick out five words within the paragraph. Then have the learners use the thesaurus to find synonyms for those words.

Test Prep

• Identifying antonyms and synonyms is an important part of preparing for standardized tests given throughout the country. Activities in this section give the learners an opportunity to deal with the subject matter presented in state-mandated tests.

Different Audiences

• When working with accelerated learners, provide them with words that have a wide variety of antonyms and synonyms and then challenge them by having them cite as many as possible.

Group Activity

• Create a game show. Divide learners into teams of two players. Each team will have one round of play. Give the first player from each team a list of words. Have the first player say words out loud one at a time. The second player then has to come up with opposite words in a set amount of time. Whichever team comes up with the most antonyms wins.

Like Words

Name _______________________

All in the Same Family

Synonyms are words that mean the same thing.
Example: Abundant and plentiful are synonyms.

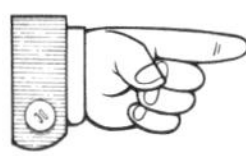 **Directions: Read the sentences below. Match the word in bold to its synonym in the word list. Write the matching synonym on the line next to the sentence.**

| response | story | led | doctor | pledge | discussion |

1. The **conversation** in the next room kept getting louder. _______________

2. He demanded an **answer** to his questions. _______________

3. The police **escorted** the criminal away. _______________

4. The **surgeon** was called to the hospital. _______________

5. The **legend** told of a time long ago. _______________

6. He took an **oath** to tell the truth. _______________

 **Pick your favorite time of year. Now think of three words to describe why you like this time of year so much. Write down those words and then find their synonyms.**

Like Words

Name ___________________________

Two of a Kind

Synonyms are words that mean the same thing.
Example: Delay and pause are synonyms.

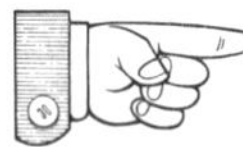

Directions: Look at each numbered row and circle the words that mean the same things.

1. portrait   religion   picture   attitude

2. classic   comedy   adolescent   juvenile

3. slender   valuable   thin   retreat

4. convict   mask   declare   disguise

5. organization   chamber   party   reception

Look around the room you are sitting in. Pick three objects and then think of a synonym for each object.

12

Name ___________________________

Opposites Attract

Antonyms are words with opposite meanings.
Example: Gigantic and *tiny* are antonyms.

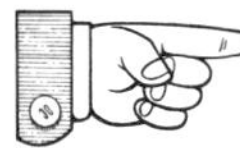

Directions: Read the sentences below. Match the word in bold to its antonym in the word list. Write the matching antonym on the line next to the sentence.

future	kind	careless	neat	harsh

1. The weather was **pleasant**. ___________________________

2. She was a very **messy** housekeeper. ___________________________

3. Dan kept thinking about the **past**. ___________________________

4. The driver was very **cautious**. ___________________________

5. Jon was **cruel** to his little sister. ___________________________

Think of three words that describe your classroom. Now come up with antonyms for those words.

Name ______________________________

A World of Difference

Antonyms are words with opposite meanings.
Example: Easy and *difficult* are antonyms.

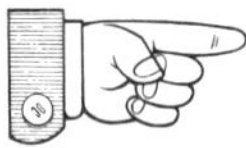 **Directions: Draw a line to match the antonyms.**

Column A	Column B
rough	energetic
scarce	allow
distant	smooth
lazy	close
forbid	plentiful
rear	joy
sorrow	front

 **Write sentences using the words in Column A. Then rewrite the sentences using the antonyms from Column B.**

14

Name ________________________

Skill Check—Antonyms and Synonyms

Like Words

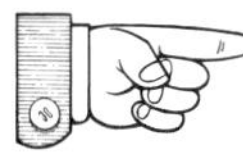 **Directions: Circle the words in each numbered row that have the same meaning.**

1. inquire   innocent   question   balance

2. true   genuine   ability   young

3. distant   condition   far   dislike

Words That Are Opposite

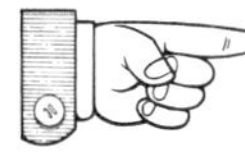 **Directions: Read the sentences below. Match the word in bold to its antonym in the word list. Write the matching antonym on the line next to the sentence.**

modern   neat   wonderful

1. It had been a **dreadful** day. ________________

2. It was an **ancient** story. ________________

3. His room was very **messy**. ________________

For *Word Meaning*
(pp. 17–21)

Background
- Multiple word meaning activities reinforce the learner's understanding of homographs. This knowledge of word variables increases learners' reading and writing abilities. By reading adjacent sentences, learners determine word meanings, preparing for future success in their own writing.

Homework Helper
- Choose several paragraphs from the learner's favorite book. Then choose several words within the paragraph that the learner is unfamiliar with. Ask the learner to read the paragraph in order to infer the meanings of the words you selected.

Research-based Activity
- Have the learner research a topic on the Internet. Next, have the learner print out three to four paragraphs of their research that contain words they are not familiar with. Then have them underline the clue words and sentences in the paragraphs that can be used to reveal the meanings of the words.

Test Prep
- The activities in this section focus on practicing inference skills. These skills are necessary for reaching state standard requirements.

Different Audiences
- Help a learner for whom English is a second language (ESL) by having him or her practice the activities in his or her language first. Then provide extra clues in each sentence to help them become more confident when contextualizing meanings for English words.

Group Activity
- Creating a memory game can help learners understand multiple meanings. Have the group draw pictures on cards of things that use the same word but have different meanings. Have the children match up the cards by figuring out the multiple meanings.

Name ______________________

Different Meanings

Sometimes a word can have more than one meaning and still have the same spelling.

Example: The word *grade* can mean the class you are in at school or it can mean the mark you got on a test.

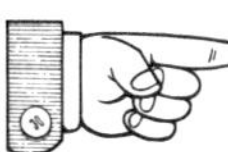

Directions: Read the sentences below. Pick the word that best fits the meanings of both sentences.

glare	trunk	state	tie	purse

1. This is a part of the United States.

   It also means to say something. ______________________

2. This can be a strong look you give someone.

   It can also be something the sun causes on a window. ______________________

3. This is something in the back of a car where you store things.

   It is also something an elephant has. ______________________

4. You can do this with your lips.

   You can also put your change in it. ______________________

5. You can wear this around your neck.

   You can also do this with your shoelaces. ______________________

Look through the dictionary to see if you can come up with two words that have multiple meanings. Write down a sentence for each meaning. You should have four sentences.

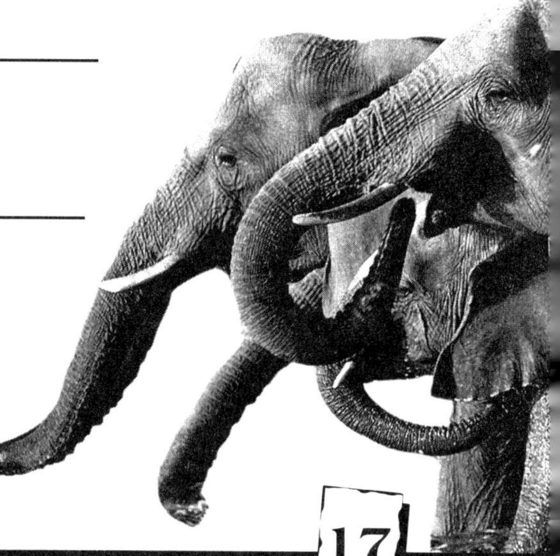

17

It's All in the Meaning

Sometimes a word can have more than one meaning and still have the same spelling.

Example: The word *fan* can mean a machine that cools a room or it can mean a person who admires someone or something.

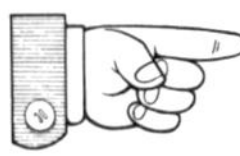

Directions: Draw a line from the sentence on the left to the sentence on the right that describes the same word. Use the word list below to help you.

bolt	coach	bark	plot	poker

A game that you play

A horse-drawn wagon

Something a dog does

A metal pin used to fasten something

A piece of land

To give instruction to

This is found on a tree

To move suddenly

This is the main story in a book

Something used with a fireplace

Come up with four words that have multiple meanings. Ask a friend to guess the word you are thinking of by giving him or her clues.

Name ______________________

What Is the Meaning of This?

Sometimes you can determine the meaning of a word by reading the sentences around it. This is called reading in context.

Example: The new girl at school was very *insecure*. She was unconfident that anyone would like her. From this sentence you can tell that the word *insecure* means unsure.

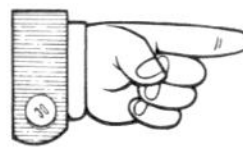

Directions: Determine the meaning of the word in bold by reading the surrounding sentences. Write the meaning of the word on the line below the sentence.

1. Eleanor Roosevelt was known for her **integrity**. She stood up for what she believed in and she was always fair.

   ____

2. Eleanor got involved in **politics**. She was very interested in the government and the law.

   ____

3. She saw much **destruction** during World War I. Many homes had been destroyed.

   ____

4. Eleanor Roosevelt **inspired** many people to stand up for their beliefs. She influenced people to make good choices.

   ____

Pretend you are teaching a class about reading in context. Pick three new words that you just learned and write a story using those words. Make sure to give clues in the story to explain the meaning of the words you chose.

19

Name _______________________

Searching for Clues

Sometimes you can determine the meaning of a word by reading the sentences around it. This is called reading in context.

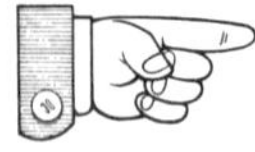

Directions: Read the paragraph below. Write down the meaning of the underlined words using the sentences in the paragraph as clues.

Oak trees can live for hundreds of years. If they are burned down, they will send up new <u>sprouts</u> from their roots. These shoots grow into new trees. Around the world people grow oak trees and <u>harvest</u> them as a crop. They gather these trees to use as wood for fire. Many oaks grow in <u>tropical</u> areas that are known for having hot climates. Oaks survive by collecting water and other <u>nutrients</u> from the soil.

1. sprouts:____

____

2. harvest:____

____

3. tropical:____

____

4. nutrients:____

____

Explain what it means to use vocabulary in context.

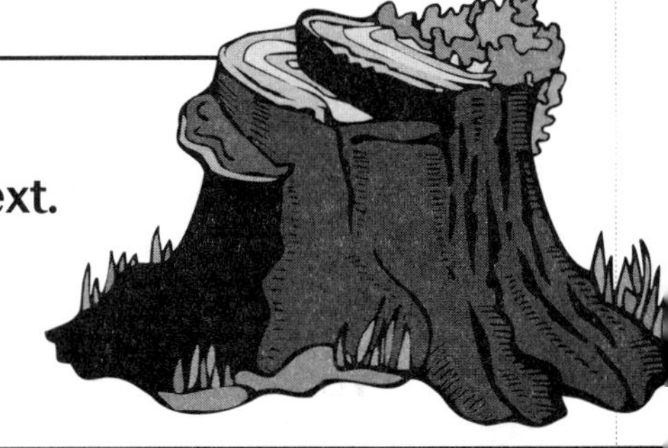

Name _______________________

Monday 4/20/09

Skill Check—Word Meaning

Multiple Meanings

Directions: Read the sentences below, then choose the word in the box that fits the meaning of both sentences.

fall	strike	watch

1. This is something you wear on your wrist.

   It is also something you can do with your eyes. ___________________

2. This is a time of year.

   It is also something that happens when you trip. ___________________

3. You do this when you hit something. ___________________

   It is also a term used in baseball. ___________________

Vocabulary in Context

Directions: Determine the meaning of the underlined word by reading the surrounding sentences.

1. It was a serious day. Everyone was very <u>solemn</u>. No one spoke very much.

   solemn:___________________

   ____

2. There were many <u>obstacles</u> to get through. The course was very challenging.

   obstacles:___________________

   ____

**For *Decoding Words*
(pp. 23–27)**

Background

- By mastering prefix and suffix recognition and comprehension the learner will vastly increase his or her ability to deconstruct words that combine a root with a prefix, a suffix, or more elaborate combinations of the two. It is important for learners to use their knowledge of word parts to determine the meaning of unknown words.

Homework Helper

- Write down a list of both prefixes and suffixes in a box. Have the learner give two words for each prefix and suffix. Ask the learner to say the words out loud to reinforce what they have learned.

Research-based Activity

- Have the learners use the dictionary to make a list of ten different words they find that either have a prefix or a suffix.

Test Prep

- Learning prefixes and suffixes gives the learner the skills necessary to decode unknown words, increasing his or her level of reading comprehension and basic word fluency. These skills will greatly enhance the learner's test-taking abilities.

Different Audiences

- For advanced learners, challenge them by providing them with difficult words. See if they can come up with the meanings of the words just by looking at the root words and the prefixes and suffixes.

Group Activity

- Have one learner pick a prefix or a suffix. Then have the rest of the group come up with as many words as possible that the prefix or suffix can be appropriately added to. Write down every word they suggest and then ask them to use the words in sentences.

Prefix

Name ___________________________

In the Beginning

A prefix is a group of letters added to the beginning of a word that changes the meaning of that word.

Example: Adding the prefix *non* to the word *sense* makes the word *nonsense*.

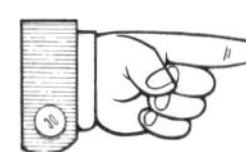

Directions: Complete the sentences by adding one of the following prefixes to the bold word listed after the sentence.

un	re	pre	mis	in

1. Carol ___________________ the question.   **understood**

2. She was ___________________ of the answer.   **sure**

3. Carol had to ___________________ the homework assignment.   **read**

4. She did not like to get an ___________________ answer.   **correct**

5. She would have to look over the ___________________.   **test**

Using the prefixes in the box above, make a list of 10 words that contain them.

Name _______________________

A New Kind of Word

A prefix is a group of letters added to the beginning of a word that changes the meaning of that word.

Example: Adding the prefix *dis* to the word *locate* makes the word *dislocate*.

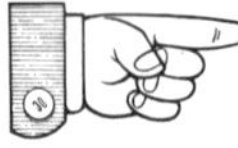

Directions: The word scramble below is full of prefixes and common words. Draw a line from the prefix to a word to make a new word. Some prefixes may be used more than once.

change

re

work

school

dis

ex

pre

un

correct

obey

place

kind

mis

in

After you have matched the prefixes to the words above, write a sentence for each new word.

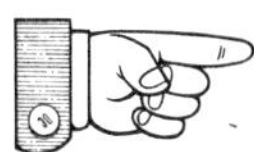

Name ___________________________

Happy Endings

Suffixes are letters added to the end of a word that change the meaning of the word.

Example: Adding *ing* to the word *trade* makes the word *trading*.

Directions: Choose two suffixes from the box that can change the meaning of the words below. Write the two new words on the lines.

able	ly	er	ful	est	ing

1. interpret ___________ ___________

2. resolve ___________ ___________

3. harsh ___________ ___________

4. fond ___________ ___________

5. prompt ___________ ___________

Choose one form of each new word you have made and write it in a sentence.

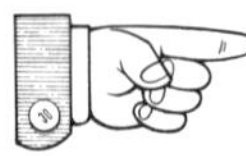

Name ___________________________

Monday 4/27/09

Last But Not Least

Suffixes are letters that are added to the end of a word that change the meaning of a word.

Example: Adding *ful* to the end of the word *hope* makes the word *hopeful.*

Directions: Read the sentences below. Then underline the suffix that appears in each one.

1. It is an adjustable wrench.

2. We are bracing ourselves for a harsh winter.

3. She casually walks over to him.

4. The termites were damaging the house.

5. The glass is extremely fragile.

6. He was the fiercest sports star.

7. Steve is looking for the perfect home.

8. She felt like the luckiest girl in the world.

26

Tuesday 4/28/09

Name _______________________________

Skill Check—Decoding Words

Prefix

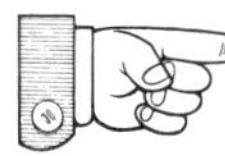 **Directions: Add the best prefix or prefixes to each word to create a new word.**

re	mis	un

1. lucky _______________________

2. fill _______________________

3. place _______________________

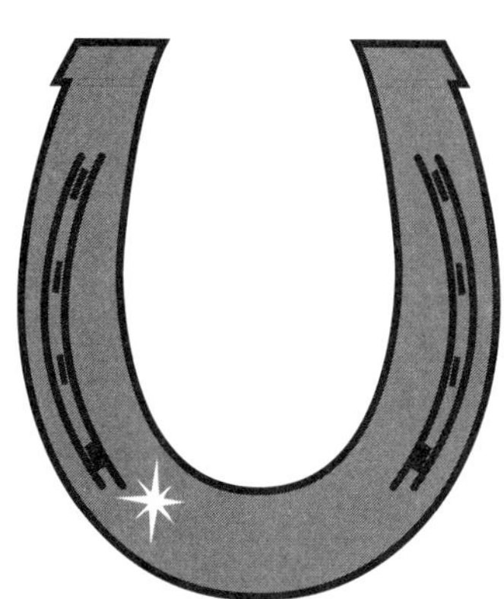

Suffix

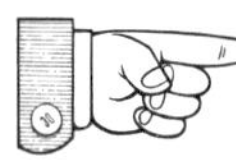 **Directions: Add a suffix to each word to change the meaning of the word.**

ing	ful	est

1. dark _______________________

2. miss _______________________

3. thought _______________________

For *Origins* (pp. 29–33)

Background

• By taking a closer look at the meaning and origins of root words and word parts, the learner becomes more adept at decoding unfamiliar words. This skill allows the learner to approach new words with a clearer understanding of word structure, making it possible for him or her to decipher the meaning of new and more difficult words.

Homework Helper

• Expand on Getting to the Root of It (p. 31) by creating more lists of root words and their definitions. Then ask the learner to come up with as many words as possible that stem from your root words.

Research-based Activity

• Using the encyclopedia, ask the learner to look up the meaning of etymology and write a short paragraph explaining it.

Test Prep

• By understanding the fundamentals of how language works, increasing an overall vocabulary, and building abilities to infer word meanings, learners increase their vocabulary fluency, making them stronger, more proficient test takers.

Different Audiences

• Have accelerated learners focus on more complex words such as those dealing with health and anatomy. By researching the Latin and Greek origins of such words, the learner will also be building on his or her science knowledge.

Group Activity

• Assign a state name to each child. Have the children do research on the origin of the state name and write a paragraph about it. Then have them read the paragraph out loud.

Name _______________________

Wednesday 4/29/09

Where Does It Come From?

Many of the words we use come from other languages. Understanding the origin of a word is important to understand its meaning.

Example: The state name of Utah comes from the Ute tribe. In the Ute language the word means "people of the mountains."

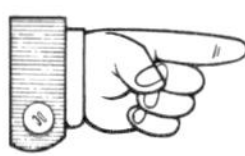 **Directions: Read the sentences and answer the questions below.**

The state name of Florida comes from Spanish, meaning "feast of flowers."

The state of Kansas takes its name from the Sioux Indian word meaning "people of the south wind."

The state of Georgia is named after King George II of England.

The state name of Minnesota comes from the Dakota Indian word meaning "sky-tinted water."

The state of New York was named in honor of the Duke of York.

1. Identify two states that are named after people.

   _______________________ and _______________________

2. What is the Dakota word for "sky-tinted water?"

   ____

3. From what language does the state of Florida takes it name?

   ____

4. From what Indian tribe does the state of Kansas get its name?

   ____

Name _______________________

Thursday 4/30/09

The Origin of Words

Many of the words we use come from other languages. Understanding the origin of a word is important to understand its meaning.

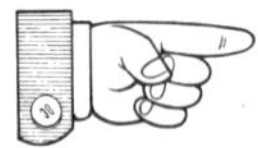

Directions: Read the passages below and then answer the questions that follow.

1. Have you ever walked into a library and wondered where the word *library* came from? It comes from the Latin word *liber,* meaning "to peel." Before there was paper, books were written on the inner bark of trees. So, the bark had to be peeled before it could be used.

   A. What did people write on before there was paper?_______________

   B. What is the Latin word for "to peel"? _______________

2. In Latin, the word *excappare* means "out of cape." This is because the ancient Romans used to throw off their capes when running from an enemy. This helped them avoid being captured. From this we get our word *escape.*

   A. Why did the Romans throw off their capes?

   ____

   B. What language does the word *escape* come from?

   ____

Name _______________________

Getting to the Root of It

Some words are made up of a root word and a prefix or suffix. To understand the meaning of this type of word, it is important to be able to identify its root. *Example:* In the word allowance, the root word is *allow*.

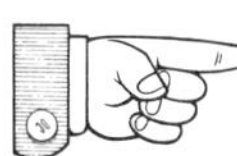

Directions: Look at the underlined word in each sentence below. Then write the root of the word on the line provided.

1. Bob has a great <u>personality</u>. _______________________

2. Judy had an <u>extraordinary</u> day. _______________________

3. Joe helped the <u>tourist</u> find the hotel. _______________________

4. The weird event seemed <u>paranormal</u>. _______________________

5. He stared in <u>disbelief</u>. _______________________

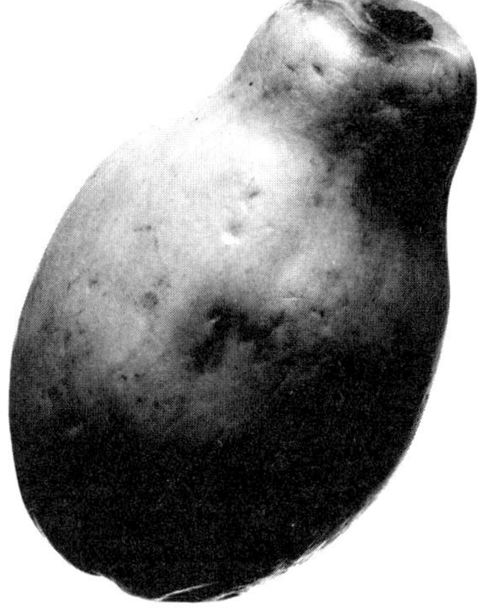

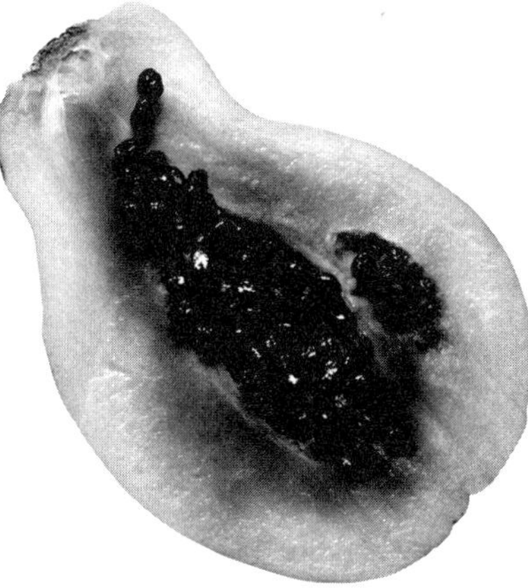

Think of two words that end with the suffix *logy* and write down their meanings.

Tuesday

Name ______________________

Setting Down Roots

Some words are made up of a root word and a prefix or suffix. To understand the meaning of this type of word, it is important to be able to identify its root.

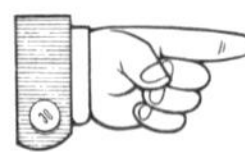

Directions: Underline the root of each word in Column A. Then match that word to its meaning in Column B.

Column A	Column B
gleeful	to enclose
attachment	to be joyous
betrayal	to separate
assistance	bravery
containment	to double-cross
departure	to fasten to
discourage	to help

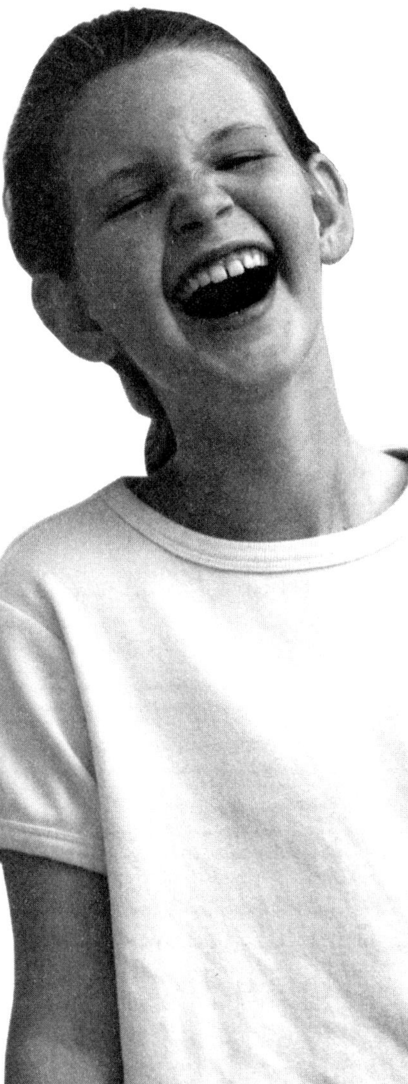

Choose three root words from this activity. Then think of as many different words you can make by adding prefixes and suffixes to your root words.

Name ___________________________

Skill Check—Origins

Word Origins

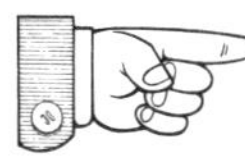 **Directions: Read the sentences below, then answer the questions.**

Today, when we vote for something, it is called casting our ballot. The word *ballot* comes from the Italian word *ballotta*. Italian citizens used to throw small pebbles, or *ballotta*, into boxes to vote.

1. What did Italian people do when they voted? _______________________

2. Where do we get the word *ballot* from? _______________________

Roots

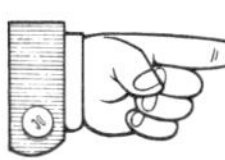 **Directions: Look at the underlined word in each sentence below. Then write the root of that word on the line provided.**

1. Judy was <u>careless</u>. _______________________

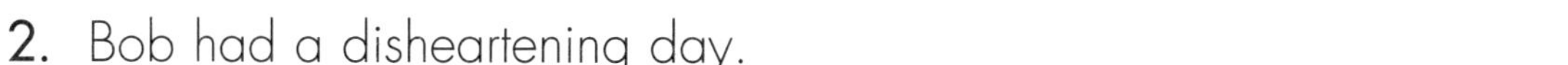

2. Bob had a <u>disheartening</u> day. _______________________

For *Figurative Expressions*
(pp. 35–39)

Background

• Learners who can make connections between different concepts through metaphors and similes will develop strong descriptive reading and writing skills. The activities in this section expand the learners' vocabulary and give them an opportunity to be more creative in their own writing by providing them with the tools needed to be more expressive.

Homework Helper

• Create a list of qualities that descriptions can be based on, such as color, size, texture, etc. Then ask your learners to pick five of their favorite things. Have them incorporate the descriptive qualities from your list into metaphors and similes to describe their items. For example, the learner might make a simile such as "the bus is as yellow as a banana."

Research-based Activity

• Have learners search in the encyclopedia or on the Internet for the term "dead metaphor." Once they understand what a dead metaphor is, have them think of as many of these common metaphors as possible.

Test Prep

• The vocabulary skills involving similes and metaphors build the learner's reading comprehension and writing proficiency, allowing him or her to be more confident when challenged with standardized tests.

Different Audiences

• Provide special-needs learners with pairs of objects that have obvious similarities such as a red balloon and a red ball. Then have them draw the connections between the objects by writing out similes.

Group Activity

• Have the learners sit in a circle. Pick a sentence to start off a simile. Have someone pick the ending. Example: The sun is like a ______.The first person to come up with an answer gets to present the next sentence. Keep going around the room until everyone has had a chance to come up with a simile.

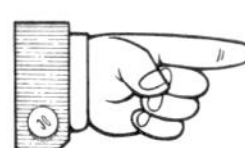

Name ______________________________

Let's Compare

> Similes use the words *like* or *as* to compare two things.
> *Example:* He was as quick as a fox.

Directions: Draw a line under the two words being compared in the sentences below.

1. The ballerina danced like a butterfly.

2. The singer's voice was as smooth as silk.

3. Tina's humming was as loud as an engine.

4. The baby slept like an angel.

5. The stranger was as cold as steel.

6. The girl sang like a sparrow.

7. Joe was as timid as a mouse.

Think of three sentences using *like* or *as*.

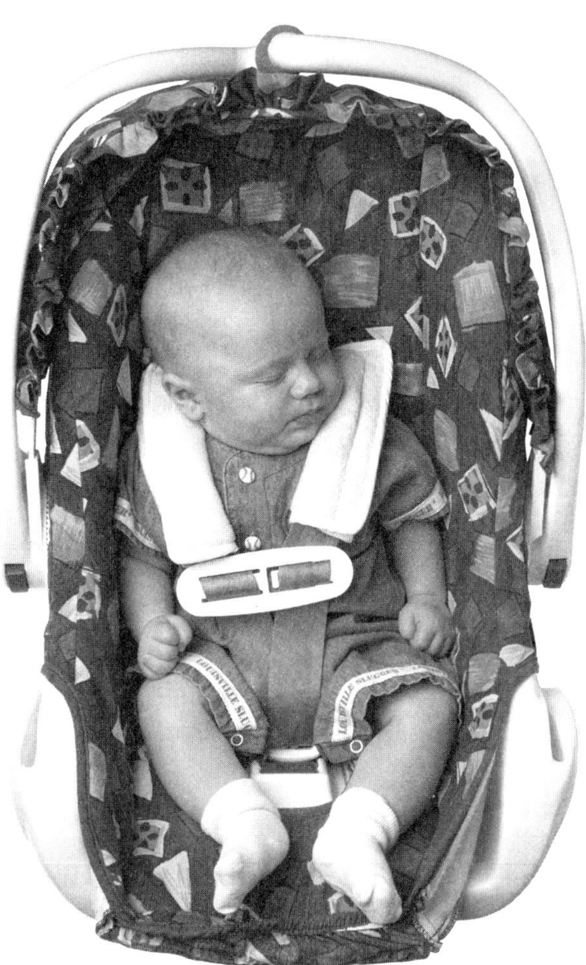

35

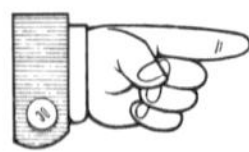

Name _______________________________

Monday

Compare This to That

Similes use the words *like* or *as* to compare two things.
Example: She is crazy like a fox.

Directions: Choose your own simile to complete each sentence.

1. The tiger's eyes shone like _______________________.

2. The puppy is as cute as a _______________________.

3. She was as happy as a _______________________.

4. He was like a _______________________.

5. John was as slow as _______________________.

6. She was as strong as a _______________________.

7. Ann could swim like a _______________________.

Pick two objects around the room, and then compare them to something else using like or as.

Metaphor Madness

A metaphor describes a thing by stating that it is another thing.
Example: The *rainbow* was a *giant painting* in the sky.

Directions: Underline the metaphor in the sentence.

1. Joan was a graceful gazelle dancing about.

2. The clouds were cotton balls in the sky.

3. The snow was a soft blanket on the ground.

4. The man was a hungry wolf when his dinner finally came.

5. The ocean was a wall between her and her true love.

6. Steven was a cat ready to pounce.

7. The stars were pinholes in the sky.

Think of three sentences using metaphors.

37

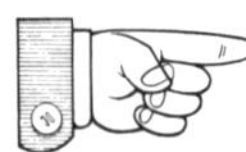

Name _________________________________

Wednesday

More Metaphors

> A metaphor describes a thing by stating that it is something else.
> _Example:_ The _bunny's tail_ was _a ball of cotton._

Directions: Choose the metaphor that best completes the sentence.

ribbon	wizard	sunshine	air	dungeon	machine

1. You are a ray of ________________ in the dark night.

2. The road was a winding ________________.

3. He is a ________________ at math.

4. Lee was a tireless ________________ working on that project.

5. Jane was so happy she was walking on ________________.

6. Matt's basement was a dark ________________.

Using the words _bird_, _rock_, and _flower_, create three sentences that use metaphors.

38

Name ___________________________________

Skill Check—Figurative Expressions

Metaphors

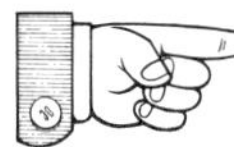

Directions: Complete the metaphor by choosing the best word to complete the sentence.

scratching	painted	rainbow

1. The different colored flowers were a __________________ in the garden.

2. The wind was __________________ at the door, trying to get inside.

3. Her face was a __________________ picture.

Similes

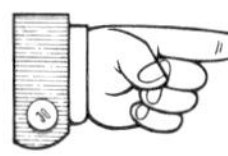

Directions: Fill in the blank with a word that completes the simile.

1. The dog barked like a __________________.

2. She was as quiet as a __________________.

3. The rocks tumbled down the mountain like a __________________.

**For *Vocabulary Helpers*
(pp. 41–45)**

Background

- The dictionary and thesaurus are invaluable resources for expanding vocabulary and reinforcing word usage skills. Learners who are familiar with these tools become more self-sufficient in their abilities to expand their vocabulary and language arts skills.

Homework Helper

- Expand on A Guiding Hand activity (p. 42) by creating several sets of guide words and a large list of words ordered randomly. Then have your learners match each word from the randomly ordered list to the set of guide words to which they belong.

Research-based Activity

- Provide learners with five sentences, each having one word underlined. Then have them use the thesaurus to look up the underlined words, choosing appropriate synonyms that could replace these words.

Test Prep

- Following written directions and feeling comfortable with multiple choice options are essential to taking standardized tests. This section provides opportunities to enhance both these skills while working on widening learners' vocabulary range.

Different Audiences

- For learners for whom English is a second language (ESL), expand on the activity on page 41 by inviting them to use a language translation dictionary to reinforce their understanding of the English word.

Group Activity

- Divide learners into two groups to play a game. Provide the two groups with words that are new to them. Have players from each group use dictionaries to find definitions of their new words. The first group to find all the definitions wins.

Name _______________________________

Look It Up

Dictionaries help you find the meaning of a word. All words in a dictionary are in alphabetical order.
Example: If you look up the word *communicate* under C in the dictionary, you will see that it means to talk or discuss.

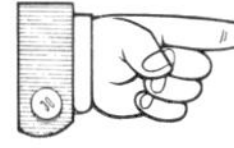

Directions: Look at the words in the box below. Use a dictionary to look up their meanings. Then match the words to the meanings below.

allowance	degree	ecology	escort	foreign

1. A person gets this when he or she graduates. _______________________

2. To lead somewhere _______________________

3. A certain amount of money given to a person _______________________

4. From a country outside of one's own _______________________

5. The study of the environment _______________________

Find three words in the dictionary you don't know the meaning of. Write the words and their meaning on paper and then memorize them.

Name ______________________________

A Guiding Hand

The words at the top of each page in a dictionary are called guide words. They are the first and last words on each page.

Example: The words *gauntlet* and *gel* could be the guide words at the top corner of the page in the dictionary that lists the *G* words that begin *gau* to the ones that begin *ge*.

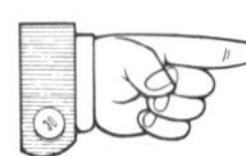 **Directions: Put the words in the box in alphabetical order between the guide words, *large* and *left*.**

last	law	late	lead	ledge	leaf	latch

large

1. ________________

2. ________________

3. ________________

4. ________________

5. ________________

6. ________________

7. ________________

left

 **Create your own dictionary page using guide words of your choosing.**

Name ______________________

Using the Thesaurus

Same Meaning, Different Word

A thesaurus is a book that lists different words that have similar meanings.
Example: hard: difficult, tough

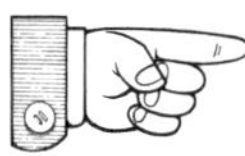

Directions: On the lines below, circle the words that might be found in a thesaurus that mean the same as the word in bold.

1. **hat:** bonnet harp cap door

2. **giant:** enormous germs huge spirit

3. **recognize:** understand identify accept rescue

4. **lumber:** blend logs lonely wood

5. **growl:** guest dark bark roar

6. **clash:** harsh conflict fight go

7. **admire:** adore smudge cherish wish

8. **vibrant:** awful bulk bright dynamic

Create your own minithesaurus. Think of three words and write down two other words that mean the same thing.

Name ___________________________

Make It Interesting

> A thesaurus is a book that lists different words that have similar meanings.
> *Example: consult:* advise   ask   confer

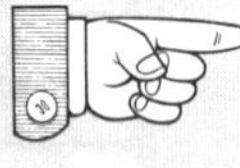

Directions: Read the story below. Make it more interesting by replacing the word in parentheses with another word that means the same thing. Look in your thesaurus for help.

Bruce woke up (happy) _________________ this morning. He (looked)

_________________ outside to see what the weather was going to be like.

The sun was (shining) _________________. It was going to be (hot)

_________________ .He was going to take his bike out and have some

(fun) _________________. Bruce enjoyed the (long) _________________

days of summer.

Make up your own story and then replace certain words to make it more interesting.

Name ________________________

Skill Check—Vocabulary Helpers

Using the Dictionary

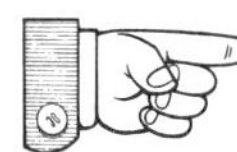 **Directions: Look up the meanings of the words below. Match the meanings to the sentences.**

recover	melody	reception

1. A formal party ________________________

2. A song or a tune ________________________ 

3. To find or get back ________________________

Using the Thesaurus

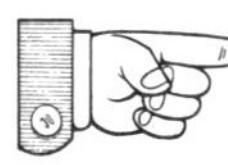 **Directions: Circle the words that mean the same thing as the word in bold.**

1. **lessen:**   reduce   add   basis   shorten

2. **conduct:**   manage   nature   ongoing   operate

3. **attractive:**   clumsy   beautiful   combine   pretty

Answer Key

p. 4

1. adored
2. conversation
3. moved
4. valued
5. flowers

p. 5

The space in a building between two floors — bank

Something that can be read in a book

A group that plays live music — snap

Something that people wear in their hair

A dog might do this if he's angry. It is also used to close things. — band

A river has one of these. It's also a place to put your money. — story

When you write your name you do this. — sign

You can read this on a wall.

p. 6

1. able
2. able
3. ful
4. er
5. ly

p. 7

1. music
2. comment
3. form
4. peddle
5. trick

p. 8

Sentences 1, 3, 4, 5 use similes.

p. 9

1. abandon
2. assemble
3. dispute
4. district
5. former
6. framework
7. perfume
8. prairie
9. preserve

p. 11

1. discussion
2. response
3. led
4. doctor
5. story
6. pledge

p. 12

1. portrait/picture
2. adolescent/juvenile
3. slender/thin
4. mask/disguise
5. party/reception

p. 13

1. harsh
2. neat
3. future
4. careless
5. kind

p.14

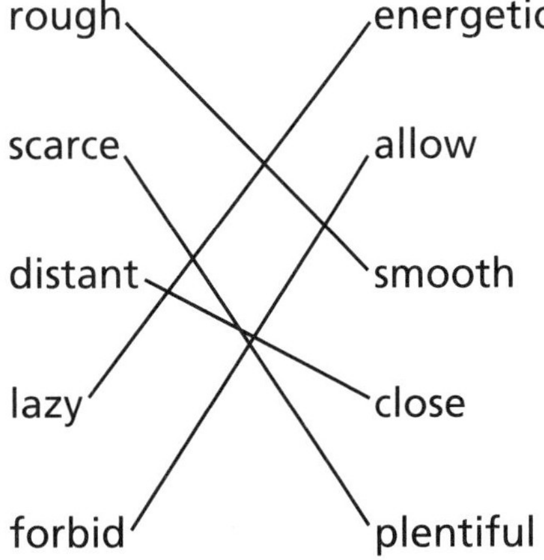

p. 15

Like Words

1. inquire/question

2. true/genuine
3. distant/far

Words That Are Opposite
1. wonderful
2. modern
3. neat

p. 17
1. state
2. glare
3. trunk
4. purse
5. tie

p. 18

A game that you play — To give instruction to

A horse drawn wagon — This is found on a tree

Something a dog does — To move suddenly

A metal pin used to fasten something — This is the main story in a book

A piece of land — Something used with a fire place

p. 19
1. Integrity is to be fair or truthful.
2. Politics involves government and laws.
3. Destruction means to ruin or destroy.
4. To inspire is to influence.

p. 20
1. shoots; a new or young plant growth
2. gather; collect
3. hot climates
4. something needed to stay strong and healthy

p. 21
Multiple Meanings
1. watch
2. fall
3. strike
Vocabulary in Context
1. grave or very serious
2. challenges; things that get in your way

p. 23
1. misunderstood
2. unsure
3. reread
4. incorrect
5. pretest

p. 24

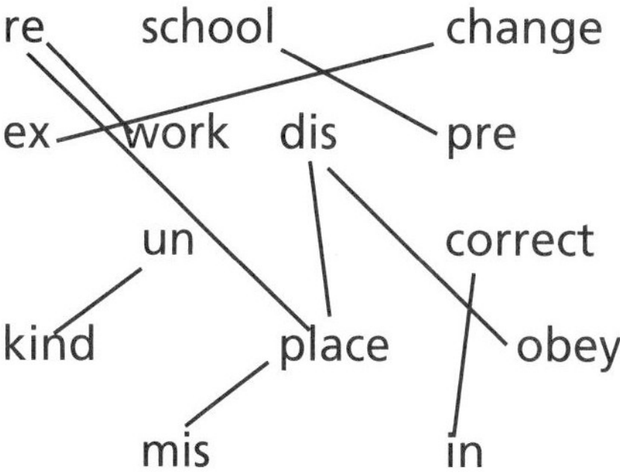

p. 25
1. interpreting, interpretable
2. resolvable, resolving
3. harshly, harsher, or harshest
4. fondly, fonder, or fondest
5. promptly, prompter, promptest, or prompting

p. 26
1. adjust<u>able</u>
2. brac<u>ing</u>
3. casual<u>ly</u>
4. dama<u>ging</u>
5. extreme<u>ly</u>
6. fierc<u>est</u>
7. look<u>ing</u>
8. lucki<u>est</u>

p. 27
Prefix
1. unlucky
2. refill
3. misplace or replace
Suffix
1. darkest
2. missing
3. thoughtful

p. 29
1. Georgia, New York
2. Minnesota
3. Spanish
4. Sioux

p. 30
1A. bark
 B. liber
2A. to escape
 B. Latin

p. 31
1. person
2. ordinary
3. tour
4. normal
5. belief

p. 32
gleeful — to be joyous
attachment — to fasten to
betrayal — to double-cross
assistance — to help
containment — to enclose
departure — to separate
discourage — bravery

p. 33
Word Origins
1. threw pebbles into boxes
2. Italian

Roots
1. care
2. heart

p. 35
1. ballerina   butterfly
2. voice   silk
3. humming   engine
4. baby   angel
5. stranger   steel
6. girl   sparrow
7. Joe   mouse

p. 36
Answers will vary.

p. 37
1. gazelle
2. cotton balls
3. blanket
4. wolf
5. wall
6. cat
7. pinholes

p. 38
1. sunshine
2. ribbon
3. wizard
4. machine
5. air
6. dungeon

p. 39
Metaphors
1. rainbow
2. scratching
3. painted
Similes
Answers will vary.

p. 41
1. degree
2. escort
3. allowance
4. foreign
5. ecology

p. 42
1. last
2. latch
3. late
4. law
5. lead
6. leaf
7. ledge

p. 43
1. bonnet, cap
2. enormous, huge
3. understand, identify
4. logs, wood
5. bark, roar
6. conflict, fight
7. adore, cherish
8. bright, dynamic

p. 44
Answers will vary.

p. 45
Using the Dictionary
1. reception
2. melody
3. recover
Using the Thesaurus
1. reduce/shorten
2. manage/operate
3. beautiful/pretty